Mathew Brady's
Photographic Studio

Cornerstones of Freedom

The Story of

THE ELECTION OF ABRAHAM LINCOLN

By Zachary Kent

Illustrated by Ralph Canaday

CHILDRENS PRESS ®

CHICAGO

Library of Congress Cataloging-in-Publication Data

Kent, Zachary.
  The story of the election of Abraham Lincoln.

  (Cornerstones of freedom)
  Summary: Follows Abraham Lincoln's political career
from his senatorial campaigning in Illinois to his early
actions as president, discussing his political opponents
and the state of the American government at that time.
  1. Presidents—United States—Election—1860—Juvenile
literature. 2. Lincoln, Abraham, 1809-1865—Juvenile
literature. 3. United States—Politics and government—
1857-1861—Juvenile literature. [1. United States—
Politics and government—1857-1861. 2. Lincoln, Abraham,
1809-1865. 3. Presidents] I. Title. II. Series.
E440.K46 1986   324.973'07   85-23274
ISBN 0-516-04669-1

9211661

Unfinished Capitol building in 1861.

The sky was bright and sunny but the air was raw and cold in Washington, D.C. It was Inauguration Day, March 4, 1861. More than 25,000 people packed the city to see Abraham Lincoln become the sixteenth president of the United States. There was a rumor that he would never live to take the oath of office. Assassins, it was whispered, planned to murder him. Many Americans were nervous and fearful about the future of the country.

The entire parade route down Pennsylvania Avenue was protected by the army. Riflemen crouched on the roofs of the houses. Infantrymen lined the road. In the side streets cavalrymen on horseback waited for danger. Even a battery of light artillery was prepared for action.

At the time of the inauguration the United States was in danger of being split in two. Already seven Southern states had left the Union. No longer would they submit to the laws of the United States, which they believed were unfair. With good reason, President James Buchanan would soon say to Lincoln at the White House, "If you are as happy, my dear sir, on entering this house as I am in leaving it and returning home, you are the happiest man in this country."

Still, Inauguration Day was a day of excitement. Music blared from marching bands and handsome floats rolled past the crowds. At the Capitol, Mrs. Lincoln and other well-dressed ladies stepped from a door and took their seats on the wooden platform. They were followed by President Buchanan, Abraham Lincoln, and several important senators. One of the senators was Stephen Douglas. He was the principal candidate Lincoln had defeated in the presidential election. They all sat down, and Lincoln prepared to give his inaugural speech. He lay his cane under his seat and then took off his tall, black, stovepipe hat. For a moment he hesitated, unsure of

what to do with it while he spoke. Then Douglas stepped forward and said, "Permit me, sir." He took the hat and respectfully held it on his lap.

To everyone who watched, this was a symbolic act. It showed that Lincoln's greatest rival was now willing to become his loyal supporter. Though Douglas and Lincoln had been political opponents for many years, they both believed that the United States must survive its present crisis. The Union must be saved. In the days ahead the nation would face the most difficult test in its history.

Long before the presidential election of 1860, people in Illinois had known who Abraham Lincoln was. Six feet four inches in his stockinged feet, Lincoln was honest, strong, and simple in style. Around the potbellied stove in his Springfield, Illinois, law office, he told jokes and stories that kept his listeners shaking with laughter.

Born in Kentucky in 1809, Lincoln spent his boyhood years in Indiana. In 1830 he followed his family to Illinois and settled there. Rising from backwoods poverty, he worked long hours as a farmhand, splitting the fence rails that would one day make him famous as "The Railsplitter." After short periods as a store clerk, a surveyor, and a small-town postmaster, he finally became a country lawyer. As an attorney Lincoln was clever and knew how to present an argument. Always interested in politics, he won a seat in the state legislature and also served a term in the United States Congress.

Stephen Douglas was well known in Illinois, too. Douglas stood only five feet two inches tall, but he was nicknamed the "Little Giant." When Douglas gave a speech, his powerful, deep bass voice sent his words crashing out like cannonballs. Douglas came from Vermont to Illinois as a nearly penniless young man. He worked as an auctioneer, a schoolteacher, and a lawyer before getting into politics. He was a natural politician, serving as a legislator, a land commissioner, and a state supreme court judge. At thirty he was elected to Congress and became a senator at thirty-four. By 1860 Douglas was the best-known senator in all of the United States.

Abraham Lincoln and Stephen Douglas first met as young men in 1834. They had been friendly rivals ever since. Lincoln once borrowed $167 from Douglas and later paid it back. In 1839 Miss Mary Todd of Kentucky came to live with her sister in Springfield. Both Lincoln and Douglas courted her and escorted her to parties and balls. When someone asked which of the two she would choose for her husband, she answered, "The one that has the best chance of being president." In 1842 Mary Todd and Abraham Lincoln were married. It would be many years before her guess would prove itself correct.

During those years when Abraham Lincoln and Stephen Douglas were growing into men in Illinois, the country was growing as well. In the North, railroads were being built and improved. Factories were going up, and thousands of immigrants were entering the country to work in them. Steam locomotives belched smoke as they carried produce from one industrialized city to another. In the South, cotton was the major crop. It was grown on large plantations worked by black slaves. In the growing season, the slaves bent among the stalks all day long, picking the raw cotton and filling up their masters' heavy sacks. The Southerners depended very much on slavery for the success of their agricultural economy.

To many the idea of slavery was tragic. The Declaration of Independence had granted the rights of "life, liberty and the pursuit of happiness" to all. But slaves were denied these basic freedoms. In 1852 a

gentle New England woman named Harriet Beecher Stowe wrote a novel called *Uncle Tom's Cabin*. It described the hardships of slavery. Thousands of Northerners who read the book were persuaded that slavery was immoral. In Massachusetts a newspaper editor named William Lloyd Garrison said that slavery was a sin and should be outlawed. Garrison and others who wanted to do away with slavery were called abolitionists. One longtime abolitionist, Senator Charles Sumner, made an insulting antislavery speech. The next day Congressman Preston Brooks of South Carolina attacked Sumner with a cane. He beat Sumner until the cane broke and the senator was unconscious.

In the South many other men were quick to defend slavery. Senator Louis Wigfall of Texas said, "I am a plain, blunt-spoken man. We say that man has a right to property in man. We say that slaves are our property." Angry Southerners like Senator Wigfall came to be known as "Fire-Eaters."

The slavery question drove a wedge between the North and South. As new lands west of the Mississippi River were settled, the argument raged: "Should slavery be allowed there?" In the Kansas Territory violent clashes erupted between bands of ruffians, some who wanted slavery and others who opposed it. The entire territory came to be known as "Bleeding Kansas." One proslavery group in Kansas carried a banner proclaiming:

Let Yankees tremble, abolitionists fall;
Our motto is, Give Southern rights to all.

While blood spilled among the Kansas settlers, the country's attention shifted to the 1858 senatorial campaign waged in Illinois. The campaign pitted Abraham Lincoln, a Republican, against Democrat

Stephen A. Douglas. History remembers this political contest for its series of face-to-face confrontations known as the Lincoln-Douglas Debates. The two adversaries met seven times in seven Illinois counties.

Standing together on a speaker's platform, Lincoln and Douglas made a striking contrast. Short and thickset with a large, round head, Stephen Douglas had a fierce, bulldog look. Tall and thin, Abraham Lincoln often looked awkward on the speaker's platform. His clothes always seemed to hang loosely on his long, narrow frame. When the excited Little Giant spoke, his words boomed loudly over the audience. By contrast, Lincoln's voice was high and calm, but people seemed to hear him much more clearly. At the debates Douglas argued that Lincoln was an abolitionist and a danger to the country. In simple and forceful language Lincoln replied that the real danger was slavery itself. Earlier he had warned, "A house divided against itself cannot stand. I believe this government cannot endure permanently half slave and half free." Reporters in the crowds took down every word the two men said. Soon their speeches appeared in newspapers all over the country.

In the end Lincoln lost the Senate election by a very narrow margin. But he managed to joke about it. He said he felt like the boy who stubbed his toe. "It hurt too bad to laugh, and he was too big to cry." He failed to realize that the debates had made him famous. Throughout the country people were asking, "Who is this man Abraham Lincoln?"

During the months following the debates Lincoln continued to travel and speak against slavery. In the Midwest, New England, and New York City he addressed crowds of eager listeners. His persuasive talks won him new admirers everywhere he went.

The winter of 1860 finally turned to spring. The time came at last to choose candidates to run for president. The Democrats and the Republicans in each state elected delegates to represent them at national conventions. Stephen Douglas was almost certain to be the choice of the Democratic party. In April the Democratic convention was held in Charleston, South Carolina. Charleston was a lovely little city, but it was in the very heart of the South. At the convention the delegates from seven Southern states insisted that slavery should be protected in the territories. The Northerners could not agree to that demand. The Southern delegates stormed out, and the convention was in ruins. The remaining delegates decided to hold another convention in June in Baltimore, Maryland.

At the second Democratic convention, Stephen Douglas was finally nominated to run for president. Unfortunately, many Southern delegates had refused to attend that convention. They insisted on a candidate who would represent their interests. They held a separate convention and nominated John C. Breckinridge of Kentucky for president.

Adding to this confusion was still another unhappy group of Democrats. They were from the border

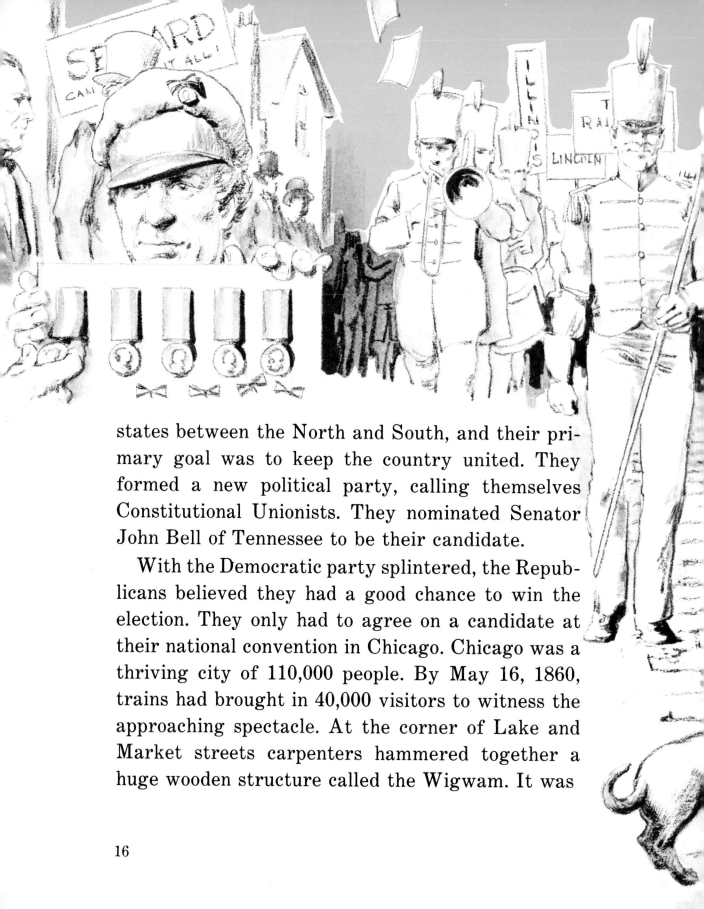

states between the North and South, and their primary goal was to keep the country united. They formed a new political party, calling themselves Constitutional Unionists. They nominated Senator John Bell of Tennessee to be their candidate.

With the Democratic party splintered, the Republicans believed they had a good chance to win the election. They only had to agree on a candidate at their national convention in Chicago. Chicago was a thriving city of 110,000 people. By May 16, 1860, trains had brought in 40,000 visitors to witness the approaching spectacle. At the corner of Lake and Market streets carpenters hammered together a huge wooden structure called the Wigwam. It was

large enough to hold 10,000 people. There the convention would meet.

Though Chicago was in Lincoln's home state, he was not expected to win the nomination. The man with the most support at the start of the convention was Senator William Seward of New York. At Lincoln's headquarters in the Tremont House hotel, secret political deals were made to get the support of state delegates. One Lincoln man was heard to say, "We are going to have Indiana for Old Abe sure." "How did you get it?" he was questioned. He replied, "We promised them everything they asked."

All of Chicago was caught up in the political whirlwind. The din of drums and bugles filled the

air. Campaign clubs marched in the streets carrying banners and emblems. Seward's supporters wore fancy ribbons on their chests and sang, "Oh, Isn't He a Darling?" Lincoln's men made a deal with the railroads. His supporters were allowed to travel to the city at a cheaper rate. Given specially printed admission tickets, they jammed the Wigwam and left little room for the Seward shouters.

On the day of the nominations, May 18, the crowd filled the Wigwam right up to the roof. Senator

Seward was nominated first and his name was greeted by tremendous cheering. Then Lincoln's man stood up. He said, "I desire . . . to put in nomination, as a candidate for president of the United States, Abraham Lincoln of Illinois." The roar from the crowd made the Wigwam tremble. One surprised reporter wrote, "Imagine all the hogs ever slaughtered in Cincinnati giving their death squeals together. . . . I thought the Seward yell could not be surpassed; but the Lincoln boys . . . made every plank and pillar in the building quiver."

The voting followed soon after. Two hundred thirty-three votes were required to win the nomination. On the first ballot Seward was given 173½ votes, while Lincoln received 102. On the second ballot the excitement increased as Lincoln's vote jumped to 181. On the third ballot Lincoln did even better. He received 231½ votes—only a vote and a half short of victory. Before a fourth ballot could be taken, several delegates changed their minds. They gave their votes to Lincoln. The tall Railsplitter from Illinois had won! All over Chicago the cry went out, "Lincoln for President! Hurrah for the Railsplitter!" Church bells rang and cannons boomed in wild celebration.

Back in Springfield, Lincoln waited calmly to learn what had happened. Finally he got the word by telegraph. Smiling, he said to friends, "I reckon there's a little short woman at our house that would like to hear the news." He hurried home to tell his wife, Mary.

Once again Abraham Lincoln was to run against his old rival, Stephen Douglas. This time, however, they were competing to become president of the United States. Lincoln was popular throughout the

North. His greatest supporters came to be called "Wide-Awakes." The Wide-Awakes organized clubs and marched in every northern city. They wore uniforms with colored capes and handsome military caps. At night they paraded the streets carrying oil-burning torches. To the music of loud brass bands they sang a campaign theme song with the words:

Old Abe Lincoln came out of the wilderness,
Out of the wilderness, out of the wilderness,
Old Abe Lincoln came out of the wilderness,
Down in Illinois.

With the Democratic party in chaos, Stephen Douglas realized his chances of winning were small. Douglas decided to do a very noble thing. Traveling all over the country, he gave speeches in favor of national unity. No matter what happened in the election, he said, the country must stay together. The Little Giant sometimes gave two or three fiery speeches a day. He spoke from the platforms of railroad cars, from hotel balconies, and at mass meetings in town squares. Once, in Montgomery, Alabama, Fire-Eaters tried to pelt him with fruit and eggs. Still, he made an eloquent speech from the steps of the state capitol.

Election day came at last on November 6, 1860. In every state, the people went to the polls and voted for presidential electors who, in turn, would vote for the president. One hundred fifty-two electoral votes were needed for a candidate to win. All day and through the night the telegraph wires hummed. When the votes were finally tallied, the results were:

	Popular Vote	Electoral Vote
Abraham Lincoln	1,866,452	180
Stephen Douglas	1,376,957	12
John C. Breckinridge	849,781	72
John Bell	588,879	39

Abraham Lincoln had succeeded. He would be the next president of the United States. He had carried all of the states in the North, as well as California and Oregon. Breckinridge had carried all of the Deep South and also Maryland and Delaware. The border candidate, Bell, had taken Tennessee, Kentucky, and Virginia. Stephen Douglas had the second largest number of popular votes. But electoral votes were what counted. He had won only Missouri and part of New Jersey.

As the news spread, Northerners rejoiced. The poet Henry W. Longfellow wrote in his diary, "Lincoln is elected.... This is a great victory.... Freedom is triumphant." Many Northerners thought that slavery would soon be abolished.

But in the South anger and despair prevailed. A Richmond, Virginia, newspaper announced, "The election of Abraham Lincoln has indeed put the country in peril." The Augusta, Georgia, *Constitution* said, "The South should arm at once." Some

Southern papers carried the election news with a black border around it, as if it were a death notice.

For many Southern Fire-Eaters, Lincoln's victory was a perfect excuse to leave the Union. The Southern states would have to secede, or break away from the rest of the country, to protect their rights and liberties. On December 20, 1860, the state government of South Carolina voted to secede. Mississippi, Florida, Alabama, Georgia, Louisiana, and Texas followed soon afterward. Meeting in a convention, they elected Jefferson Davis to be the first president of the new Confederate States of America.

In Springfield, Lincoln waited silently for the day of his inauguration. From Northerners he received many letters of congratulations. Some angry Southerners sent him hateful letters. He was called an ape and a baboon. People threatened to burn, hang, or torture him.

In early February, 1861, Lincoln traveled alone down to Coles County, Illinois, to say good-bye to his stepmother. Old Sarah Lincoln took her boy, now a great man, tightly into her arms. She cried over him and said she would never see him again. She guessed that he would be killed.

A week later, Lincoln boarded the train that would carry him from Springfield. A cold, drizzly rain fell, but a crowd gathered to say good-bye anyway. Feeling their affection, Lincoln gave a touching farewell speech. "To this place, and the kindness of these people," he said, "I owe everything.... I now leave, not knowing when, or whether ever, I may return, with a task before me greater than that

which rested upon Washington." As the train moved
down the tracks, surely many citizens of Springfield
sent their prayers traveling after it.

During the long trip to Washington, D.C., the
train stopped in town after town. In Westfield, New
York, a crowd gathered to wish Lincoln well. From
the rear platform, Lincoln asked if a certain Grace
Bedell was there. A little girl was led forward. Lincoln lifted her up and kissed her. Grace had written

him a letter suggesting that he would look more handsome with a beard. Lincoln wanted to show her that he had taken her advice. A dark black beard now fringed his lower face.

The train moved on, and within days Lincoln received distressing news. Rumors warned that he would be killed by assassins when the train reached Baltimore. His advisers insisted that he sneak through Baltimore at night on a different train. Reluctantly Lincoln agreed. At last he arrived in Washington safely. One of the first men to greet him and pledge his support was his old rival, Stephen Douglas.

On March 4, 1861, the two men shared the same platform, as they had done so often before. This time, though, the crowds had come only to hear Lincoln. Even the protective sharpshooters stationed in the Capitol windows were straining to hear his words. In his inaugural speech Lincoln called for peace and understanding between the North and the South. "We are not enemies, but friends," he said. "We must not be enemies." He insisted, though, that the Southern states obey the laws of the Constitution. The nation could not survive if broken into two separate countries.

Unfortunately, the Southerners refused to listen.
In another month the Civil War began when the
South Carolina militia fired on Fort Sumter, a Union
fort in Charleston harbor. Virginia, North Carolina,
Arkansas, and Tennessee left the Union. Lincoln
called for 75,000 volunteers to put down the rebel-
lion. These were the first of many blue-clad marching soldiers. Soon the land flashed with the gleam of
cavalry sabers. It shook with the pounding crash of
cannon fire and the shouts of dying men. The smoke

of a million muskets rolled across a hundred bat-
tlefields, places with names like Bull Run, Shiloh,
Antietam, and Chancellorsville.

At Gettysburg, Pennsylvania, in November 1863,
four months after a great battle there, Lincoln
arrived to dedicate a cemetery. Within sight of his
speaker's platform, broken caissons and discarded
rifles, knapsacks, and canteens still littered the
ground. Closer at hand, row upon row of shallow
graves were a reminder of death. Lincoln rose, tall

and worn. He spoke briefly and finished, "We here highly resolve that these dead shall not have died in vain; that this nation, under God, shall have a new birth of freedom; and that government of the people, by the people, for the people, shall not perish from the earth." Two more years of bloodshed awaited, but the United States had elected a president who would fight to the end to preserve the Union.

About the Author

Zachary Kent grew up in Little Falls, New Jersey, and received an English degree from St. Lawrence University. Following college he worked at a New York City literary agency for two years and then launched his writing career. To support himself while writing, he has worked as a taxi driver, a shipping clerk, and a house painter. Mr. Kent has had a lifelong interest in American history. Studying the U.S. presidents was his childhood hobby. His collection of presidential items includes books, pictures, and games, as well as several autographed letters.

About the Artist

Ralph Canaday has been involved in all aspects of commercial art since graduation from the Art Institute of Chicago in 1959. He is an illustrator, designer, painter, and sculptor whose work has appeared in many national publications, textbooks, and corporate promotional material. Mr. Canaday lives in Hanover Park, Illinois, with his wife Arlene, who is also in publishing.